Countries of the World: A Primary Source Journey

A Primary Source Guide to

SWEDEN

Christopher Blomquist

The Rosen Publishing Group's

PowerKids Press™

PRIMARY SOURCE

New York

For Mary Beth, who's not Swedish but who is wonderful nonetheless. Jag älskar dig!

Published in 2005 by The Rosen Publishing Group, Inc.
29 East 21st Street, New York, NY 10010

First Edition

Editor: Kathy Kuhtz Campbell
Book Design: Haley Wilson
Layout Design: Michael J. Caroleo
Photo Researcher: Adriana Skura

Photo Credits: Cover Image © Hans Strand/Corbis; p. 4 © 2002 Geoatlas, (inset) © ScanPix; p. 6 © Stone/Getty Images, (inset) © Masakatsu Yamazaki/The Image Works; p. 8 © Giraudon/Art Resource, NY, pp. 8 (inset), 18 © IBL Picture Agency Sweden; pp. 10, 14 © Lee Snider/The Image Works, (inset) © AFP/Corbis; p. 12 © Vander Zwalm Dan/Corbis Sygma, (inset) Macduff Everton/Corbis; p. 14 © Alex Farnsworth/The Image Works; p. 19 © Hulton/Archive/Getty Images; p. 20 © Lonely Planet Images.

Library of Congress Cataloging-in-Publication Data

Blomquist, Christopher.
A primary source guide to Sweden / Christopher Blomquist.
    p. cm. — (Countries of the world, a primary source journey)
Includes bibliographical references and index.
Summary: Text and photographs reveal the culture, history, artifacts, and traditions of the nation of Sweden, one of the world's northernmost countries.
ISBN 1-4042-2758-X (library binding)
1. Sweden—Juvenile literature. [1. Sweden.] I. Title. II. Series.
DL609.B56 2005
948.5—dc22

                                        2003020254

Manufactured in the United States of America

Contents

Atlantic
Ocean

Kebnekaise ▲

SWEDEN

Gulf of Bothnia

FINLAND

RUSSIA

NORWAY

Helsinki ▪

Oslo ▪

ESTONIA

Stockholm ▪

Skagerrak
○Göteborg

Gotland

North Sea

Kattegat

Öland

LATVIA

DENMARK
Copenhagen ▪

Helsingborg ○

Öresund

Baltic Sea

LITHUANIA

BELARUS

4

Where Is Sweden?

Sweden is in Scandinavia, an area of north-central Europe that includes Norway and Denmark. It lies on the eastern side of the Scandinavian **Peninsula**. Norway occupies the rest of the peninsula, to the west of Sweden. Finland borders northeastern Sweden.

Sweden has about 4,400 miles (7,081 km) of coasts. Its southwest coast faces branches of the North Sea, including the Skagerrak strait and the Kattegat strait. A strait is a narrow waterway that connects two large bodies of water. The port city of Helsingborg lies 2.5 miles (4 km) east of Denmark, across the Öresund strait. Sweden's east coast faces the Gulf of Bothnia in the north and the Baltic Sea in the south. Two Swedish islands, Gotland and Öland, lie in the Baltic Sea.

In land area Sweden is the largest Scandinavian country. It is 173,732 square miles (449,964 sq km). *Inset:* Red cottages, such as this one, are common in Sweden. The red paint is made from a metal that is dug from Falun copper mine.

The Land of the Midnight Sun

Sweden is one of the world's northernmost countries. One-seventh of its area is above the **Arctic Circle**. In Sweden's northernmost parts, the sun never rises in the winter and never sets in the summer! For this reason, this area is called the Land of the Midnight Sun.

Northern Sweden is called Norrland, or "the northland." This area occupies two-thirds of the country and is mostly covered with forests, mountains, and hills. Central Sweden, or Svealand, is an area of low, wooded plains that are good for farming. Sweden's capital, Stockholm, is on Svealand's east coast. Southern Sweden is called Götaland. This damp area has forests with rocky hills and lakes and swamps.

Kebnekaise is the highest mountain in Sweden. A peak in the Kjølen Mountains in northern Sweden, Kebnekaise is 6,965 feet (2,123 m) tall. *Inset*: A Sami girl stands next to a reindeer. The Sami people live north of the Arctic Circle.

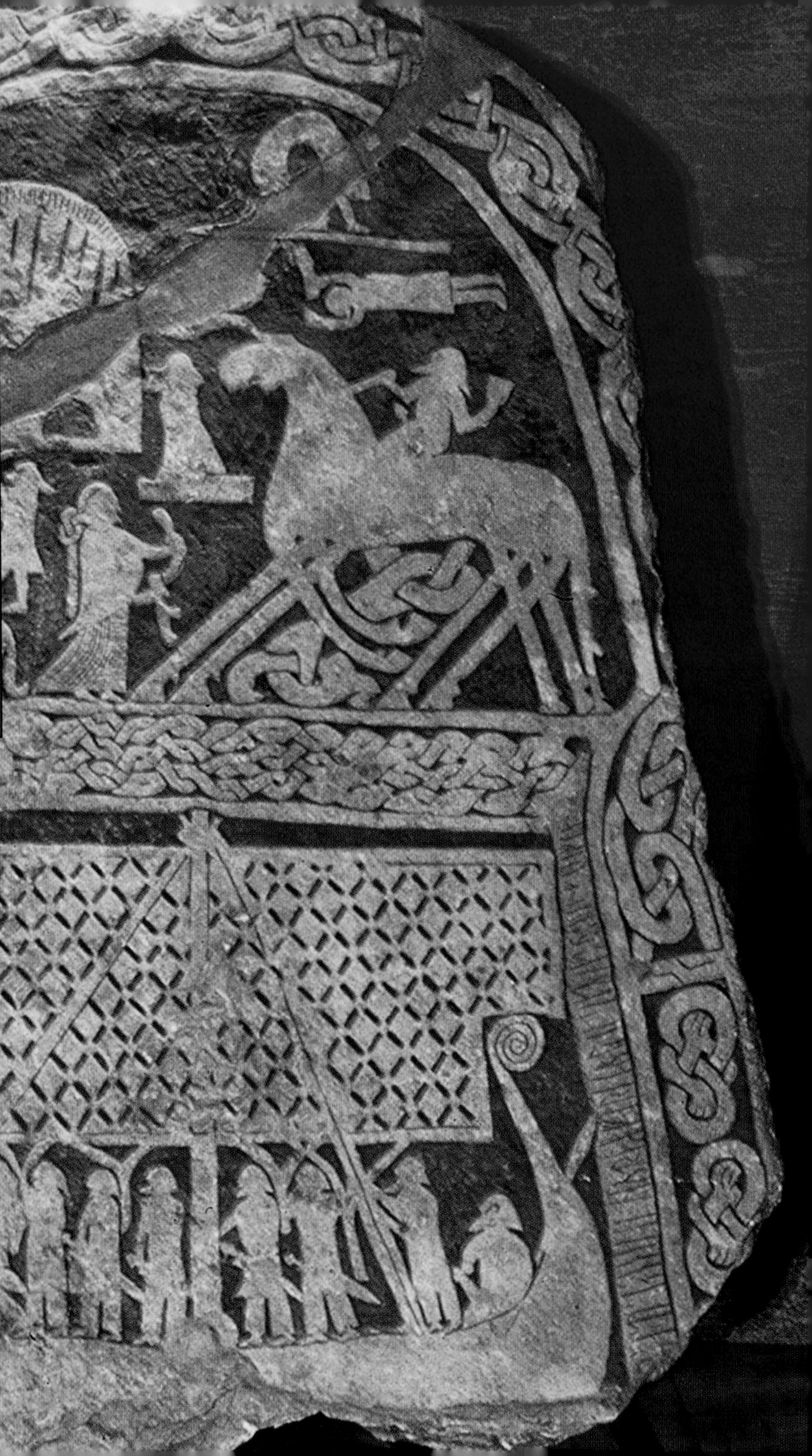

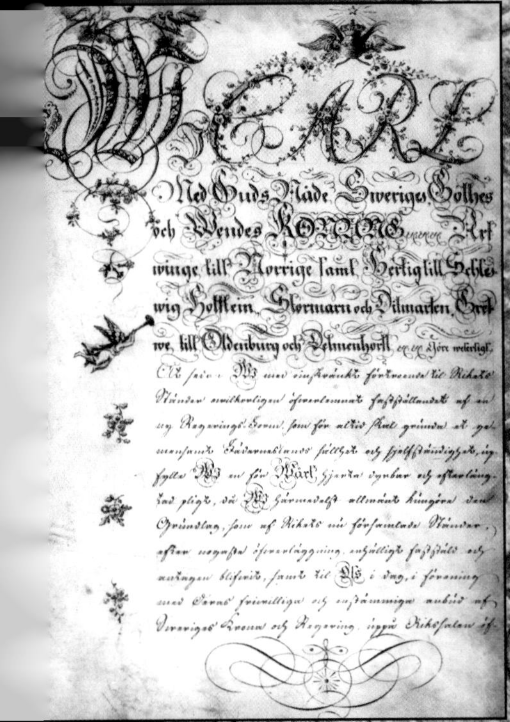

Wars and Peace

The first people to live in Sweden arrived 12,000 years ago. By A.D. 98, a tribe called the Svear lived there. The tribe's homeland was named Sverige, or "land of the Svear." Over time the name Sverige became Sweden. People called Vikings ruled Scandinavia around 770. Around 829, Ansgar, a monk from present-day Germany, began to spread Christianity throughout Sweden. Sweden crowned its first Christian king, Olof Skötkonung, around 1000. Its greatest king, Gustavus II Adolph, ruled from 1611 to 1632. Although Sweden battled countries such as Denmark over land in the 1600s, it is now **neutral**. King Charles XIV John stated its neutrality in 1834.

This stone carving from the ninth century shows a Viking ship and was found on Gotland Island. The Vikings attacked their neighbors and sailed ships all the way to southern Europe and North America. *Inset:* The constitution of 1809 stated that Sweden was to be ruled by the king using a group of advisers.

Sweden's Government

Sweden is a **constitutional monarchy**. This system of government has been in place since January 1, 1975. That is when Sweden's **constitution** went into effect. The constitution granted the right to vote to every citizen who is at least 18 years old. According to the constitution, the king or the queen is the official head of the country but has no real power. It is the **prime minister** who is in charge. He or she is chosen by a 349-member **parliament** called the Riksdag. Riksdag members are elected by Swedes who live in the country's 21 counties. Members serve four-year terms. They approve and write laws. A group of about 20 advisers, called a cabinet, helps the prime minister.

This photo shows the island of Gamla Stan, or Old Town. Stockholm, Sweden's capital, was first founded as a trading post on this island in the early thirteenth century. *Inset:* Göran Persson was chosen as Sweden's prime minister in 1996.

The Swedish Economy

Sweden depended on farming in the 1800s for its economy. Between 1868 and 1873, crops such as potatoes and wheat failed to grow in Sweden. Between 1846 and 1873, 1.5 million Swedes moved to North America. This was about one-fourth of the population. In the early 1900s, Sweden built factories in cities such as Göteborg. Swedes grew wealthy from iron and steel production. Today 2 percent of Sweden's 4 million workers farm or fish while 74 percent of them work in places such as banks and hotels. Twenty-four percent work in manufacturing, such as automobile production, papermaking, furniture making, and glassmaking.

Around 1912, Electrolux made the first home vacuum cleaner. It has a head office in Stockholm and it still makes household machines. *Inset*: This Orrefors glassblower works in a factory, one of many in southern Sweden's area called the Glass Kingdom.

Speaking Swedish

Swedish is the official language of Sweden. Swedish comes from an old language called Common Scandinavian that later branched into the Swedish, Norwegian, and Danish languages. Swedish is also related to German and English. Swedish was first spoken around 1000. Until about 1250, Swedish was written in an ancient alphabet with letters called **runes**. Today Swedish is written with the same alphabet as English, but there are 29 letters. Several Swedish sayings refer to the land's many woods and countrysides. For example, if Swedes want someone to leave them alone, they say "Dra at skogen!" which means "Be off to the forest!"

The Viking rune-stone pictured here is from the eleventh century and is located in Uppsala University Park in Uppsala, Sweden. The Vikings left hints of their arts, beliefs, and habits in the form of runes. The rune-stones were often set up as monuments for dead people, such as this one, or for a battle that had been won.

Religion in Sweden

Although about 87 percent of Swedes belong to the Church of Sweden, only about 10 percent attend church services regularly. The Church of Sweden is a **Protestant** religion called **Lutheranism**. In 1540, King Gustav I Vasa founded the Church of Sweden and made it the national religion, or way of worshipping God. In January 2000, the Riksdag granted freedom of religion to everyone.

Sweden's Christmas season begins on December 13, or St. Lucia's Day. St. Lucia was a Roman girl who was killed because she refused to marry a non-Christian. Young girls dress as St. Lucia and sing carols and visit churches, hospitals, or schools.

On St. Lucia's Day, girls, such as these in Stockholm, wear white robes with red sashes in honor of St. Lucia. Some also wear crowns with lit candles. Sometimes they are accompanied by boys wearing paper hats with stars.

Fun Stories and a Great Award

Swedish authors have written many great books. Astrid Lindgren, a Swede who lived from 1907 to 2002, is a well-known writer of children's books. In the 1940s, she wrote three books about Pippi Longstocking, a girl who wears her hair in two crooked braids. Pippi lives with her horse and monkey in a funny house and has many adventures.

Another famous author is Selma Lagerlöf, whose 1906 children's book *The Wonderful Adventures of Nils* tells of a little boy who becomes a dwarf and travels across Sweden. In 1909, Lagerlöf won writing's highest honor, the **Nobel Prize**. Prize winners get money for doing good work in the world.

This is the 1944 book cover for Astrid Lindgren's *Pippi Longstocking*. The Pippi books have been printed in about 60 languages. *Above:* Swede Alfred Nobel left money in his will for the creation of a yearly award. The Nobel Prize is awarded to people for their accomplishments in the sciences, writing, or peace.

Sweden Today

Sweden is a member of the **European Union** (EU), which it joined in 1995. Its membership in this union may force the usually neutral Sweden to take a stand on world issues. However, it has not replaced its official money, the krona, with the EU's money, called the euro.

Since 2000, a bridge and a tunnel, called the Öresund Link, have connected Sweden to Denmark, and to the rest of Europe. People used to use boats to travel there. Using cars or trains on the Öresund Link, which stretches 10 miles (16 km), has improved the travel time between the countries by 25 minutes. Swedes hope that by joining their country with the rest of Europe, they will improve economic ties as well.

The Öresund Link is made up of a bridge and a tunnel that connect Malmö, Sweden, to Copenhagen, Denmark. *Inset:* The money used in Sweden is the krona. Kronor is plural for krona. This 50-kronor note shows the nineteenth-century singer Jenny Lind, who was called the Swedish Nightingale.

Sweden at a Glance

Population: 8,888,000

Capital City: Stockholm

Largest City: Stockholm, population 743,703

Official Name: Kingdom of Sweden

National Anthem: "Du gamla, Du fria" ("Thou Ancient, Thou Freeborn")

Land Area: 173,732 square miles (449,964 sq km)

Government: Constitutional monarchy

Unit of Money: Krona

Flag: Sweden's flag is a blue rectangle with a gold cross. The gold cross is formed by two lines that meet on the left side of the flag and run to the flag's edges. Blue and gold are the colors of Sweden's national coat of arms, or special seal. The flag dates from the sixteenth century.

Glossary

Arctic Circle (ARK-tik SUR-kul) A pretend circle around the North Pole.

constitution (kon-stih-TOO-shun) The basic rules by which a country or a state is governed.

constitutional monarchy (kon-stih-TOO-shuh-nul MAH-nar-kee) A government in which a country has both a king or queen and elected leaders.

European Union (yur-uh-PEE-in YOON-yun) A group of countries in Europe that work together to be friendly and to better their businesses.

Lutheranism (LOO-thuh-ruh-nih-zum) A Protestant faith based on the teachings of Martin Luther.

neutral (NOO-trul) On neither side of an argument or a war.

Nobel Prize (noh-BEL PRYZ) An award of money given each year to a person or a group for good work in areas such as science, writing, or peacemaking. The prize is named for Swedish inventor Alfred Nobel, who established the award.

parliament (PAR-lih-mint) The lawmakers of a country.

peninsula (peh-NIN-suh-luh) An area of land surrounded by water on three sides.

prime minister (PRYM MIH-nih-ster) The leader of a government.

Protestant (PRAH-tes-tunt) Having to do with a faith based on Christian beliefs.

runes (ROONZ) An alphabet used by the Norse people between the third and the thirteenth centuries.

23

Index

Primary Source List

Cover. Sarek National Park in northern Sweden is the country's oldest national park. It was founded in 1909.

Page 4 (inset). Red cottages located throughout the country have become a national symbol for Sweden, mostly because the red paint is made from the red ore that is dug from Sweden's Falun copper mine.

Page 6 (inset). A Sami girl and a reindeer. For hundreds of years the Sami of the Norrland region of Sweden were called Lapps. Today English speakers use the term Sami, which is a variation on Sabme, the name used by Sami to refer to themselves.

Page 8. Viking rune-stone depicting ritual navigation. Ninth century. Found on Gotland Island. Statens Historiska Museet, Stockholm.

Page 8 (inset). Sweden's constitution of 1809 established a constitutional monarchy for the country. At the time, this constitution was the second oldest in the world, next to that of the United States.

Page 14. Eleventh-century rune-stone at Uppsala University Park, Uppsala, Sweden. This Viking rune-stone might have been erected by two Vikings named Tägen and Gunnar in memory of Väder, their brother.

Page 18. The original cover for Astrid Lindgren's book, titled *Pippi Longstocking*, published in 1944.

Page 19. Swedish chemist Alfred Bernard Nobel. This photo was taken around 1890, six years before the inventor of dynamite died. Nobel left $9 million in his will to create an annual prize to promote peace because dynamite was used as a weapon in war.

Web Sites

Due to the changing nature of Internet links, PowerKids Press has developed an online list of Web sites related to the subject of this book. This site is updated regularly. Please use this link to access the list:

www.powerkidslinks.com/cwpsj/pswed/